10

LITTLE RULES
for
the
Modern
Southern Belle

by Beverly Ingle

ISBN-13: 978-0-9974799-8-0

For more information visit www.10littlerules.com

dedication

For my four baby belles,
who are growing into beautiful, strong,
capable women with Modern Belle sensibilities.
I couldn't be prouder.
For Joe, who loves me immeasurably,
yet I have no idea why.
I win!

table of contents

foreword

Beverly and I connected through our work, both managing editorial teams for a dot.com back at the end of the last century. She was working remotely from Texas while I, a native New Yorker, was freshly planted in the Bay Area, the hub of internet cool.

We clicked. In fact we clicked so hard that our friendship quickly turned into something more akin to sisterhood, and when we finally met in person at an all-hands company conference, our fates were sealed. We were each other's chosen family, and always would be.

Through reorgs, downsizing, layoffs, divorces, moves, stresses, joys and sorrows, Bev gave me the gift of herself in all her sassy, smart and completely authentic self. Through her I learned the importance of the Spring Toenail Pledge, the self-affirming effect of donning lipstick for a trip to Home Depot, and the true meaning and value of a friendship that spans many years ... and many miles ... and is only the stronger for it.

Congratulations, Bev, on this book and on continuing to shine, staying grounded in your roots while evolving to your next iteration. Much love to my favorite Modern Southern Belle.

Carol

Carol Pearson
Founder, 10 Little Rules
www.10littlerules.com

introduction

Just as in life, beginnings and endings are the scariest parts. All my life as a writer, it's been the introductions and conclusions with which I have always struggled. I would sometimes beg my mom to write them for me. She never did, of course, but she had a magical way of pulling out of me exactly what I wanted to say. Sadly, she passed in 2012, so I'll sit quietly and wait for her to unlock my words ...

I have always been proudly Southern and fascinated by the curiosities of Southern culture. Not its history, mind you, for that contains some of the darkest years America has ever seen. As I write this, pacifists are protesting, rioters are looting and cities are burning in angry, aggrieved response to the systemic inequities and racial bigotry that led to another Black man losing his life needlessly ... a situation that wrested away the media headlines from the worldwide COVID-19 pandemic and is now intricately linked to an upcoming election. The irony of writing a light-hearted book about Modern Southern Belles in this time and space is not lost on me. However, this is precisely the time when we all need a little levity, a break from the madness and seriousness to have a little giggle and embrace what's beautiful about the South. And I hope you enjoy it.

Beverly Ingle

RULE #1
don't forget your lipstick

Southern style is a thing of beauty in its own lovely way, and the Modern Belle has style down pat. In no way do I intend to offend ladies of other U.S. regions, but come on. I'm willing to bet y'all don't put on lipstick before heading out to the Piggly Wiggly. Am I right?

The image most people have when they think of a belle is a dated one, featuring big hair and bold accessories. After all, it was a Southerner – albeit a transplant from the Midwest – who coined the phrase "the higher the hair, the closer to God." A non-Southerner also envisions lots of pink in our collective color wheel. Not the trendy Millennial Pink, but the bashful-and-blush type. Those may have been Shelby's signature colors, but they aren't universally loved. I, for one, look horrible in pink.

If that's your mind's-eye image of a Modern Belle, you need to poke it out with a dull pencil.

While some of us may love pink and still keep Aqua Net in business, the vast majority broke that mold a long time ago. On the outside, Modern Belles could look like anyone from anywhere. Pixie cuts, Doc Martens, jandals, natural hair or gorgeously intricate braids, a wardrobe with lots of black, messy buns, Magellan fishing shirts, Tory Burch flats, Old Navy flip-flops … the variety of style is broad

RULE #1
don't forget your lipstick

and deep, and belles embrace the opportunity to be themselves.

However, not all the rules have gone by the wayside. Pearls and diamonds are always a good choice – even with a T-shirt and jeans – and no one can rock that look better than a belle. White pants and dresses do not make their appearance before Easter or after Labor Day. White shoes do not make their appearance ever (unless they are tennis shoes).

A Modern Belle still does not step out in public without lipstick or gloss, even if the rest of her face is sans makeup. We do not skip moisturizer or sunscreen. Our shoes, belt and purse no longer match, and that's ok. (Really Mom, it's ok.) Pantyhose are reserved for formal events, if they are worn at all. Jeans are ubiquitous since you can dress them up or down. Everything fits well, because everyone knows (or is) an excellent seamstress.

And while your toenails must always be painted, they can be any crazy color you like. Toes are OPI's playground, so have fun. But for God's sake, keep those toenails painted. A naked toenail is tacky, and there's nothing tackier than being tacky. If that isn't reason enough for you, keep in mind that Southern gentlemen love that pop of bright color.

You might be thinking, "This style isn't unique to belles," and you'd be right. What is unique to the Modern Belle and what sets her apart from other women is the way she carries herself. A knowing eye can spot a belle in a crowd by her posture, confidence, manners and charm. Southern style truly is distinctive with a 'je ne sais quoi' flair.

your turn ...

don't forget your lipstick

Think about your own style for a moment. Do you take the chance to express yourself? Maybe for you it's wearing bold colors or donning jeans as sort of a personal uniform, which saves time making clothing decisions in the morning.

Or are you following rules that make no sense for you and who you want to be? What would happen if you abandoned those rules to write your own? Use the journal space on the next four pages to reflect on and write down your thoughts.

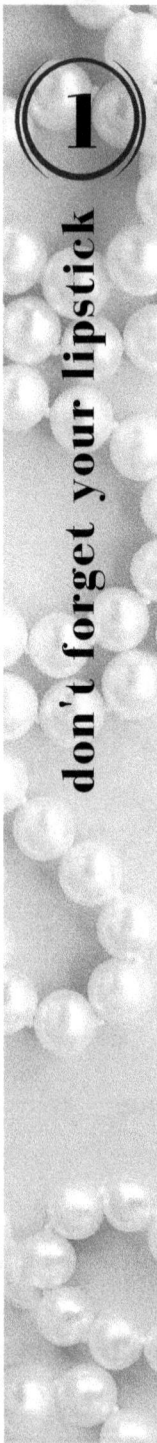

1

don't forget your lipstick

date _____

don't forget your lipstick

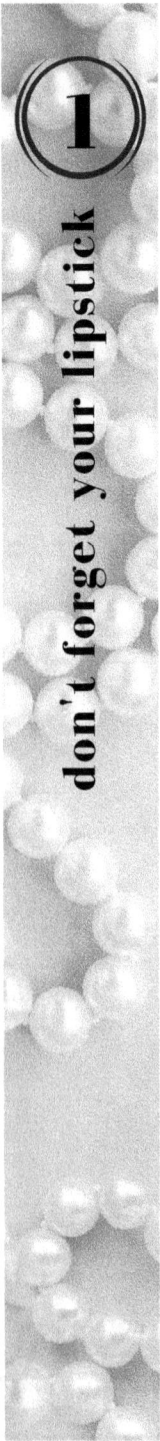

1

don't forget your lipstick

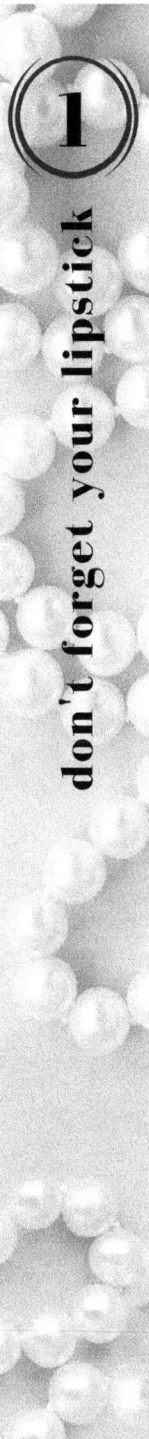

date _____

don't forget your lipstick

Beverly Ingle

RULE #2
welcomes are always warm

Pound cake. Two words that have become synonymous with hospitality in the South, and both should be served up warm.

There are scads of treasured, family pound cake recipes ... as many versions as there are versions of hospitality. Yet they all share one thing in common, and that's sweetness. The same could be said for the welcome given to strangers, friends, neighbors and family: They are inevitably sweet. Southern Belles, modern or not, show up to family events, to potlucks with friends and on new neighbors' porches with voices raised in elation, hugs all around and fresh, homemade pound cake. I have a dear friend who, when she and her husband moved to the South, gleefully looked forward to receiving warm greetings complete with a welcome-to-the-neighborhood pound cake. It was high on her list of Southern traditions she looked forward to experiencing.

(She was bitterly disappointed when it didn't happen ... until I pointed out she'd moved to a neighborhood of mostly Northern transplants whose idea of a warm welcome was a head nod and wave as they drove by. Enough said.)

Greetings reach a sometimes unexpected level of intimacy in the South, regardless of context, and even the most introverted of Modern

RULE #2
welcomes are always warm

Belles will greet you warmly. In many a board room, you're as likely to
hug hello as you are to shake hands. To a lot of people, that sounds
odd and inappropriate. Where I'm from, it's not unusual for our warm
welcomes to bleed into business, when we will greet potential clients,
bosses and colleagues for the first time with a hug. The reactions to
this among non-Southerners are certainly something to see, not that
they are cold or unemotional; they're just totally caught by surprise. A
few years ago, prior to a new business pitch, I walked into the
organization's boardroom and the vice president and I promptly gave
each other a hug hello. We'd never met before, but we were both
raised in Texas, and that's what you do. On the other hand, the look on
her French colleague's face as I went to hug him hello was
priceless! I couldn't tell if he thought I was going to punch him, harass
him, or somehow get him in trouble with his boss as well as his wife.

The warmth doesn't stop at the hug. Because most belles have huge
hearts and inquiring minds, we genuinely want to know how your mom
is doing, if you've gotten over your cold, if your kid's Little League
team won or if your vacation was all you'd hoped it would be. We'll
pepper you with questions as a means to connect and build a
relationship. We aren't being nosy. We're showing real interest in you
as a person. And we'll absolutely expect the same from you. In fact,
even if you don't ask, we'll probably share how our mom is doing, that
we beat the cold, our kid's team won and our vacation was lovely,
thank you!

The Modern Belle is all about a warm welcome. Making others feel
supported, comfortable and at ease – regardless of who they are or the
context we're in together – is a privilege, and we take it to heart.
And really, shouldn't everybody?

your turn ...

welcomes are always warm

Think for a moment about the last person you met and how you greeted him or her. Were you warm and welcoming? How do you think that made the other person feel? How did it make you feel? If you weren't as warm and welcoming as you could be, why? What is holding you back from extending your warmth and goodwill to others?

2

welcomes are always warm

date _____

welcomes are always warm

welcomes are always warm

date _____

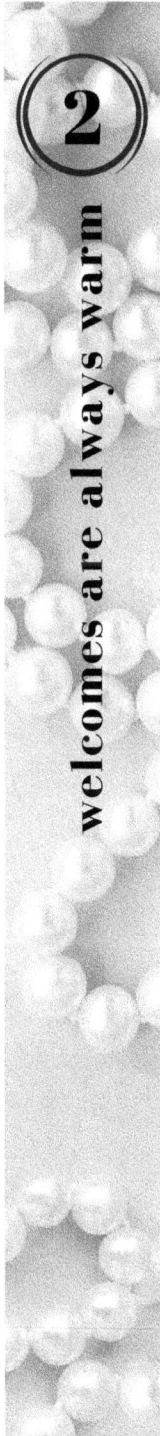

date _____

welcomes are always warm

RULE #3
food is a love language

We Southerners know how to eat and eat well. Food is a deep part of our souls, and it plays a central role in nearly every occasion. Ask any belle about a pivotal moment in her life, and she will likely recall what was served or what she ate in minute detail. And it doesn't have to be a big event to warrant careful planning and preparation of the food that accompanies the fun.

You see, food is an expression of love in many Southern households. And love, as well as a fondness for food – both eating and cooking – are a special part of life from Day One. Growing up, we all had our favorite dishes that our moms or memas cooked for us, and when they did, it was a special occasion, even if it was just a random Tuesday. As we grew older, we had the joy of learning how to make those favorites for ourselves. (It's not the same, though.)

Generations-old lessons were passed down to Modern Belles in their family kitchens, many of which were about what occasions warranted food, and what kind of food it warranted. Because not just any-old dish would do.

Deaths and new babies call for casseroles, and these are when family favorites are proudly shared. Apparently, casseroles are a Southern thing ... at least, they are according to my non-Southern

RULE #3
food is a love language

friends. As one English friend pondered, why do we find the need to put everything into the same dish? Frankly, because it's easy, can feed a crowd and usually freezes well if there are any leftovers. A newer trend a Modern Belle embraces during these occasions is delivering breakfast foods – pastries, fruit, bagels and whatnot – figuring not everyone needs a dozen casseroles nor wants to eat one in the morning. What a Modern Belle does not do is have food delivered via Postmates or Grubhub or opt for a restaurant gift card. That's just tacky and impersonal. If you don't have the time or talent to cook something yourself, at least show up in person with something yummy you picked up.

Dinner parties are a mainstay in Southern entertaining, and menus are always carefully planned. While Modern Belles aren't opposed to experimenting in the kitchen, they know some things are better left alone. For example, when it comes to the classics, the Modern Belle doesn't mess with perfection. You can show up to her dinner party without the fear of discovering that kale has replaced the spinach in her wilted spinach salad with hot bacon dressing or that she's replaced the mashed potatoes with mashed cauliflower. And if you ask her, "What can I bring?" don't be surprised if she tells you, in great detail. The Modern Belle isn't too shy to take you up on your offer.

your turn ...

food
is a love
language

Think about your own entertaining, whether for family or friends. What traditions have you incorporated, and what new ideas have you brought to the table? Are you creating your own legacy of food as a love language?

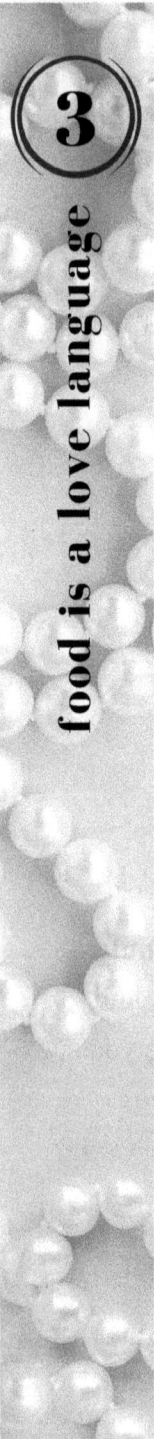

3

food is a love language

date _____

food is a love language

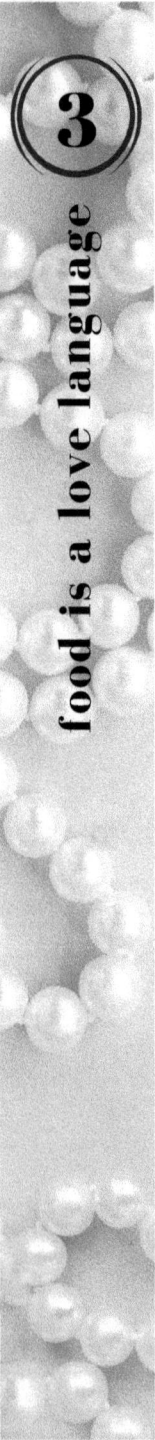

3

food is a love language

date _____

food is a love language

Beverly Ingle

RULE #4
mama knows best, sometimes

Mamas don't just hold a special place in our hearts. They also hold a unique and powerful place in the Southern home and community. Mamas are the beginnings of our worlds and our moral compasses. They are bellwethers of our futures and the founts from which we draw encouragement, strength and love.

Mamas also seem to be the keepers of all truths. This is not a surprise. There will be hundreds – if not thousands! – of times that we will say to ourselves or even aloud, "Mama was right."

Depending on your age and the circumstance, you'll find that Mama's all-knowingness is downright irritating. Yet, there will be times when you'll also find some comfort in it. In hindsight, the truths Mama shared were basically bumper guards for life. They kept you safely in the lane and moving forward. That's what Mama's goal was then, and it's her goal for you still. And for that care and devotion, we are thankful.

Let's be real though, ladies. Mama isn't always right.

She may be right about the power of a well written thank-you note, but she's not right about keeping your resumé plain and limited to one page. If you have the experience and chops, show them off in two pages; you've earned it. If you're in a less formal industry like

RULE #4
mama knows best, sometimes

communications, you know there's a vast sea of candidates competing for the job you want. So, there's no harm is designing your resumé to stand out from the crowd. After all, that's why the world has Canva.

Mama may have encouraged you to err on the demure side at work, during a conversation or while interacting with men. Oh, hell no. I mean, no ma'am, Mama. Regardless of bumper guards, if the Modern Belle wants to get to where she wants to be, she speaks up. She shares her thoughts, opinions and insights. Sure, she listens attentively to whomever she is with, but she actively engages in conversation and holds her own. And on issues she is passionate about, the Modern Belle unabashedly plants a stake in the ground and says, "This is where I stand on that topic."

Mama may have insisted that the "experts" know what they are doing, and it's not our job to question them. Nope! Wrong. Experts may know their stuff, but that doesn't mean they are impervious to mistakes. It's every Modern Belle's right to ask questions of the experts, not only for her own learning, but also as a sly opportunity to uncover what could be a pending error on the expert's part. We belles aren't in the business of embarrassing anyone, so questions could be another's saving grace when it comes to retaining that expert status.

For many Southern women, Mama, or her mama's mama, may also have been on the wrong side of history. Attitudes of racial and class bias are often passed down right along with Mama's advice on proper grooming and how to make a perfect biscuit … sometimes unspoken, sometimes blatant. The Modern Belle takes an unflinching look at this family point of view and does the hard work of calling it out in herself. She calls it out as she sees it, and works to build alliances, choosing not to keep old walls of ugliness and hate intact.

RULE #4
mama knows best, sometimes

Discovering that Mama isn't all-knowing can be a harsh reality; the fact that she isn't perfect is OK. She's an individual as much as you and I are. She's allowed to make mistakes just like we do, and the older we get, the more comfortable we are with that knowledge.

I'm a mama, too, and very much an individual. When my daughters were young, they thought I knew everything. Now they're discovering I don't always have the answers. I can remember the looks on their faces when that understanding set in. When my girls were growing up and asked questions I didn't know the answer to, I'd respond with "very carefully," "lots of practice" or "only the experts know." One of those usually satisfied their curiosity and helped me dodge a bullet. I knew the jig was up when one daughter asked how to change a tire on the car, and another daughter answered for me, "Very carefully." Busted.

However, regardless of the accuracy of my answers to their and life's questions, I will always use what I know as bumper guards for them. It's the very least I can do.

your turn ...

mama knows best, sometimes

Did you consider your mama a source of all answers when you were younger? Do you still seek her knowledge and advice now? Think about when you discovered that Mama wasn't always right. Did that change your relationship? If so, how? Are you passing on family traditions that have no place in the modern world?

date _____

4

mama knows best, sometimes

34

date _____

mama knows best, sometimes

4

mama knows best, sometimes

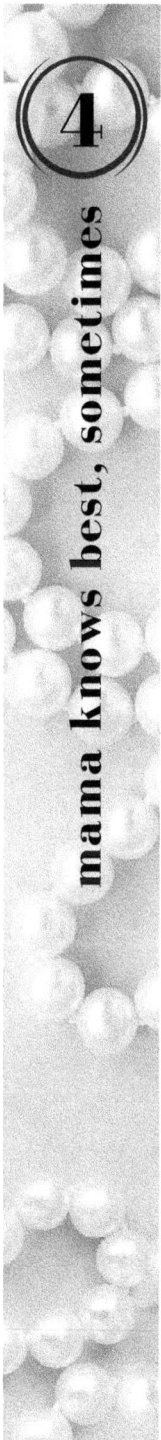

date _____

mama knows best, sometimes

RULE #5
don't hide your crazy

In the South every family has its eccentrics, to varying degrees. Growing up, the odd behavior or quirks of some of my own family members were written off as simply unique characteristics. "She's high-strung." "That's just the way Uncle Peter is." "She's down in the dumps." "He's intense."

It wasn't until I had friends who grew up in other parts of the country that I learned not every family has eccentrics. In fact, according to anyone I know who isn't Southern, most families don't. I'm pulling the bullshit card on that. Every family, in fact everyone, has some kind of crazy going on. The difference in the South is that we don't hide our crazy.

The other difference is that the crazy we put out on the front porch for all to see is the socially acceptable kind. By that I mean the kind of crazy everyone shares a giggle and knowing glance about. The real crazy remains hidden. The serious concerns about a family member's behavior are rarely discussed, and when they are talked about, it's in hushed tones behind closed doors. What would the neighbors think if they knew just how down in the dumps Aunt Sara is?

Avoiding those conversations is a huge disservice to mankind, really, because the real crazy deserves to be talked about just as much as

RULE #5
don't hide your crazy

Aunt Sara herself.

The Modern Belle isn't scared of or embarrassed by the real crazy. Hell, she's crazy herself, but opts to use the grown-up words for it. Anxious. Depressed. Manic. Bipolar. Whatever she is, she boldly and unapologetically owns it, too. This Modern Belle, yours truly, struggles with anxiety and depression. Some days or weeks are worse than others, but my kind of crazy is omnipresent, and that's just the way life is for me. I don't mind talking about it either. It makes some people uncomfortable, but more than once it's helped someone to know I was an empathetic audience with whom they could share their own crazy.

I believe a little bit of mental illness has become a fundamental part of the human condition, and the more we're willing to talk about it, the more normal it becomes. The more normal it becomes, the more likely the folks who need help will get the support that they need. Period. Getting off my soapbox now.

To my point, take a look at your social feeds sometime. A close look. I bet you'll see other Modern Belles not hiding their crazy. Whether it's a meme they've posted or a direct comment, it's there, and we all bond over it. One of my favorites is a Tweet from Josh Hara (who I'll dub an honorary belle):

> Sticks and stones may break my bones
> Words will also hurt me
> Compliments make me uncomfortable
> I have social anxiety
> I'm a wreck
> Just go

RULE #5
don't hide your crazy

Ask any one of the four friends I socialize with and they'll tell you, yes, at the last minute Bev will cancel plans she enthusiastically made weeks prior. In true Southern form, my mom would describe that habit as one of my quirks. In Modern Belle form, I don't mind saying it's just an aspect of my anxiety. <shrug>

your turn ...

don't
hide your
crazy

Who are the eccentrics in your family, and how does everyone treat them? Do you hide your own crazy? If so, what are some ways you can own it and find the support you need?

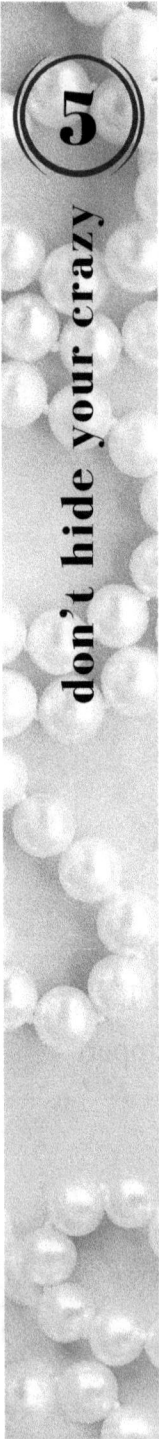

5

don't hide your crazy

date _____

don't hide your crazy

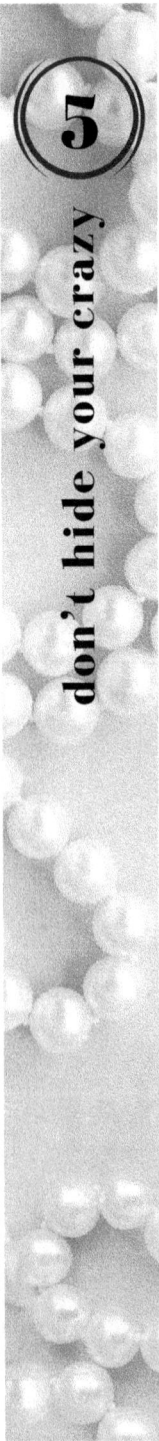

don't hide your crazy

date _____

date _____

don't hide your crazy

5

RULE #6
you can choose your family

There's no such thing anymore as an average American family (assuming there ever was). Ask most Southerners and they'll tell you they've never been average or never have known an average family. A stereotypical one, sure. But we don't do average.

Southern families are chock full of stories about crazy aunts, funny uncles, in-laws twice over, kissing cousins, married cousins, families who've kept exes and disowned the blood-relatives, high drama, ugly divorces and suspicious deaths. That's why Southern novels are equally fascinating and relatable; there's always a kernel of truth in the tale.

For all the shapes and forms family can take, there's a common thread that runs through communities and that's friends who are like family. The Chosen Family, one friend of mine called them. They can make surviving your own family and its dynamics possible, and they can give you the family you've always dreamed of. Belles have known this universal truth for generations. Modern Belles have embraced it in new ways.

I am an only child. My childhood was filled with imaginary friends and cousins. It wasn't a sad childhood, but definitely not an average or a stereotypical one. And while I loved my extended family, I

RULE #6
you can choose your family

became accustomed to creating the siblings I had always hoped for out of my friends. Wherever we went, we would tell strangers we were sisters and giggle at our secret truth.

This continued on in a way when I became a mother with young children. Since I don't have siblings and my husband's brother doesn't have kids, my own children don't get the benefit of having a cadre of aunts, uncles and cousins. Being the Modern Belle I am, I was not deterred. My and my husband's cousins became our kids' aunts and uncles. Our closest friends became their aunts and uncles, too. So what if the DNA is absent? The love and the sentiment are there ten-fold. Those people we love and cherish are The Chosen Family.

Sometimes, The Chosen includes folks you wouldn't normally expect, like an ex-husband and his new family, your husband's best friend whose wife was your husband's former girlfriend, or a colleague-turned-soul sister. In fact, one my favorite family vacations was a Disney cruise with my husband and our three daughters; my oldest daughter and her father, step-mother and half-brother; my father, my mother and my step-father; and my mother-, father-and brother-in-law. How would you like to be the waiter serving that crazy 13-person table at dinner? It wasn't the first time we were all together, either. We had the pleasure of spending holidays together quite often. It's amazing what can happen when you set aside old hurts and disappointments and instead focus on the good stuff and what's best for the kids involved.

Modern Belles aren't afraid to pick and choose who they consider family – traditional definitions be damned – and their lives are the richer for it. Shouldn't everyone's be?

your turn ...

you can choose your family

When you think about your family, who comes to mind? If they don't match the traditional definition of family, why do you consider them a part of yours anyway? If you could create your version of the perfect family, do you have everyone you want in your life right now? Who's missing?

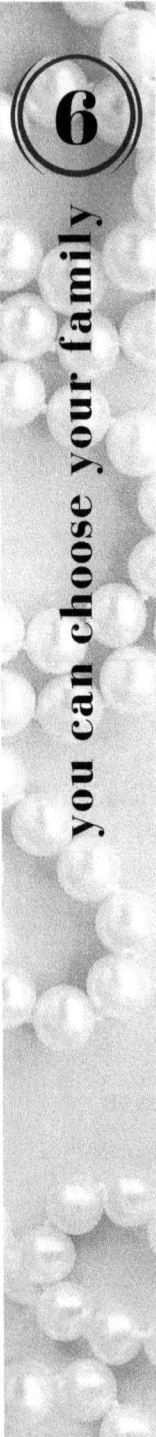

6

you can choose your family

date _____

you can choose your family

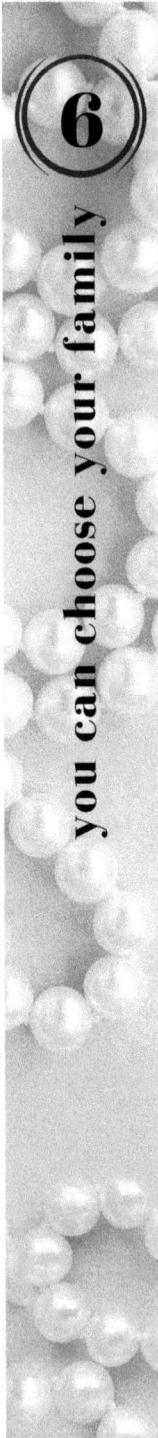

6

you can choose your family

date _____

you can choose your family

RULE #7
mind your ma'ams and sirs

There's a summer camp nestled into the Texas Hill Country that has hosted generations of children and teens and helped nurture them into respectable young men and women. During the personal interview part of the application process, a child's ability to demonstrate good manners carries a lot of weight with the camp leadership. Informally referred to "ma'ams and sirs," the manners the camp's leadership expect to see go well beyond the proper use of honorifics; they're also looking for a general display of kindness, consideration of others and at least a smattering of proper etiquette. Based on what I've witnessed over the past couple of decades from the sidelines of my children's lives and through my own experiences, I would imagine that camp's average attendance is in jeopardy.

Using good manners is rapidly disappearing as quickly as a wildfire consumes the California landscape. Why is that? Theories abound, but I think my late mother said it best when she declared, "There's a total lack of consideration of others out there in the world." And truly, that's what it boils down to, because if you can show some consideration, good manners naturally follow.

I have to wonder, though, is this decline the beginning of the end? Not if we do something about it.

RULE #7
mind your ma'ams and sirs

So, what is the Modern Belle to do? Take the bull by the horns. Show her mettle and live by example. It doesn't get more basic than that. Consider this...

The modern Southern Belle like you and me holds the door open for strangers, no matter their gender or age. This is not difficult. As you pass through a doorway, simply hold the door open behind you for a little longer than you normally would. It takes all of three seconds, and the person behind will inevitably appreciate the gesture.

On public transportation, give your seat to your elders, pregnant women and anyone else who would seem to benefit from sitting more than you would. Even if your feet ache from breaking in your new Louboutins, you know that if you were in the other person's shoes (pun intended), you'd be grateful for a chance to sit.

This next part is fundamental. Please pay attention. Aside from our ability to accessorize, what separates us from men and animals is this: A belle never forgets to say hello, please and thank you to wait staff, doormen, postal workers, delivery drivers and janitors. Working in jobs that are critical to a civilized society, many people often go overlooked and under-appreciated, and that's a true shame. It's said that if you want to know how a man will treat his wife, look at how he treats his mother. I'd say if you want to know about a belle's character, look at how she treats the postman.

Further, the Modern Belle is always pleasant to children and dogs because neither can comprehend why an adult could be surly in a world full of wonder (at least as seen through their eyes).

Consideration of others is the embodiment of The Golden Rule – do unto others as you would have done unto you – and that consideration extends beyond the moments that obviously require good

RULE #7
mind your ma'ams and sirs

manners. What about when crossing a busy street or even an aisle in a parking lot? The modern Southern Belle doesn't saunter. She steps up her pace in order to cross as quickly as possible. Changing lanes while driving? She uses her turn signal – gasp! – and then waves a quick thank you to the driver behind who let her move over. She will even sometimes mouth or say aloud thank you in the silence of her own vehicle.

The modern Southern Belle respects personal space. You won't find her practically standing at your elbow in line at the Piggly Wiggly or curiously eyeing the screen of your mobile phone. There's this notion of a personal bubble, and she knows not to step into yours. However, if you're reading Southern Living next to her on the plane, she totally has the right to read over your shoulder.

Along those same lines, she completely understands the unspoken social contract that applies to conversations in public places like coffee shops, restaurants, subway cars, planes and any queue that requires more than a three-minute wait. It is fascinating to me the things other people will discuss in public places, assuming that others are ignoring them. Nope. Fortunately, though, the Modern Belle may eavesdrop to her heart's content, but it goes in one ear and out the other, never to be repeated to another soul. And she damn sure won't post what she's heard on social media. Speaking of...

Social media demands consideration and civility. Just because a conversation happens online doesn't mean all decorum can be thrown out the window. You must still be respectful and tactful, which is incredibly hard when you vehemently disagree with someone's perspective and aren't looking them in the eye. As a rule of thumb, if you wouldn't tell someone they're an idiot to their face, don't

RULE #7
mind your ma'ams and sirs

do it online. If you would tell them to their face, then shame on you.

And for goodness' sake, think twice before you post something online anywhere and if you're going to tag someone else, you'd better ask first. Not everyone wants the world to know where they were having dinner and with whom on Saturday night. Digital content has the potential to live forever, and as we've seen in recent political and celebrity news, even a years-old comment or appearance at an event can come back to haunt you. The old adage remains true: if you wouldn't want your mema to see, read, hear or know it, don't share it!

So, from doorways and dining out to coffee shops and changing lanes, life hands us Modern Belles plenty of opportunities to practice good manners. It's so much more pleasant when we all mind our ma'ams and sirs, don't you think?

your turn ...

mind your ma'ams and sirs

Think of some occasions where your or someone else's manners were lacking or even nonexistent. What could you have done differently? How would that have possibly changed the experience and/or the outcome?

mind your ma'ams and sirs

date _____

date _____

mind your ma'ams and sirs

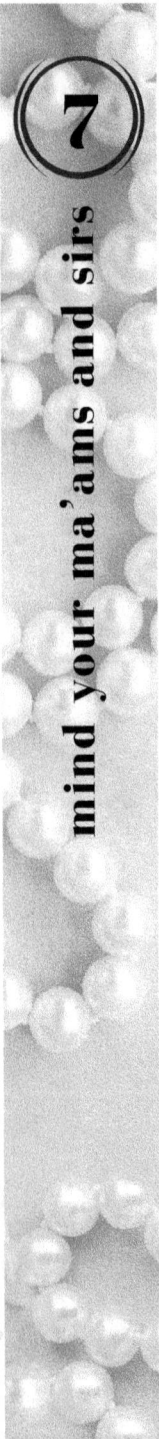

mind your ma'ams and sirs

date _____

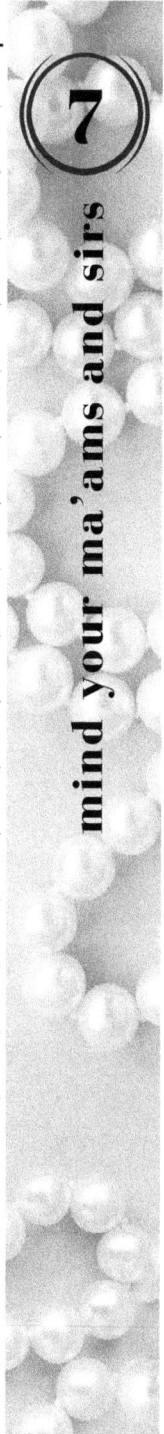

date _____

mind your ma'ams and sirs

RULE #8
practice sass with class

"If you can't say something nice, sit by me."

I absolutely love that line from Clairee in Steel Magnolias. Its sass elicits laughs, but it's the nuance of that sass that gets to the heart of social commentary in the South. It's sass with class. It isn't crude, rude or hurtful, but simply honest and straightforward. With someone like Clairee, you know exactly what she means.

Being sassy is as much a part of being Southern as knowing the difference between y'all and all y'all. (I once tried to explain the differences among you, y'all and all y'all during a keynote presentation at a conference in Poland. I can't imagine the struggle the translator must have gone through.)

Let me be clear though: Sassy is never, ever mean. The Modern Belle is not a Mean Girl. She does not malign others, and she doesn't always wear pink on Wednesdays. Quality sass has class and style and wit. Sass is also more of a character trait and less of an attitude. Bitchy is an attitude. There's a distinct difference.

The Modern Belle knows how to be sassy in the most delicious way. She leverages her sense of humor and eye for irony to sling her sassiness, and people tend to respect her perspective and honesty. One of the best compliments I ever received was in a gift from a dear

RULE #8
practice sass with class

cousin, a refrigerator magnet that reads, "I try for sweet but sassiness always slips out."

Modern Belles embrace clever turns of phrases and lace them with the perfect amount of sass. When done well, friends are impressed and gentlemen stand in awe. A quick Pinterest search will yield tons of sassy statements, but few with the class of a Modern Belle. I've chosen a select few not only to share why they are classy, but also to give you some fabulous fodder for your most dynamic conversations.

The absolutely best and most recognizable bit of Southern sass is this: Bless her heart. Let me break it down for you.

The meaning is totally dependent upon the tone and context. "Bless her heart" can be a sincere expression of concern. It can be a shared laugh about someone else's silliness. Or it can be a scathing send-up worthy of Julia Sugarbaker. Along the same lines is "bless her baby heart," which typically takes on a tone of pity.

Similar to bless her heart is any statement that starts with honey, as in "Honey, let me tell you something ..." In that context, the recipient better watch out because some criticism is about to be let loose on you and, most likely, you deserve it. In contrast, a belle might use honey as a term of endearment. Believe me, you'll know the difference when you hear it.

Falling into the same category of the sassy-but-classy honey are also lovely, darling and precious, which aren't always compliments. Conversely, there's ugly. Now, if you hear a belle tell her child, "Don't be ugly," don't stand there looking aghast. She isn't commenting on the child's physical appearance, but rather his or her behavior. Ugly is a Southern synonym for rude or mean, and using it is much classier

RULE #8
practice sass with class

than scolding your child in front of your minister. Because the Modern Belle knows not to be ugly herself.

As you can see, the common threads throughout Southern sassiness are the tone in which the words are said and the context in which they are used. Pay attention the next time anyone says to you, "Well, bless your heart," and you'll know whether to respond with "Don't be ugly" or "Thank you."

your turn ...

practice
sass
with class

When was the last time you let loose with the sass? Would you describe it as a Modern Belle moment, or was it a flash of Mean Girl instead? Think of some situations when you wished you had spoken up or spoken out, but instead remained silent. How would you handle that now?

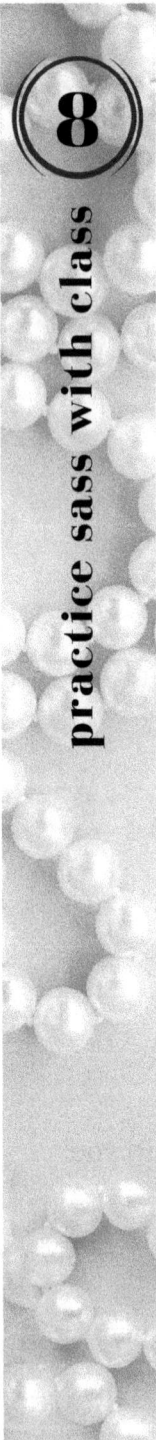

8

practice sass with class

date _____

practice sass with class

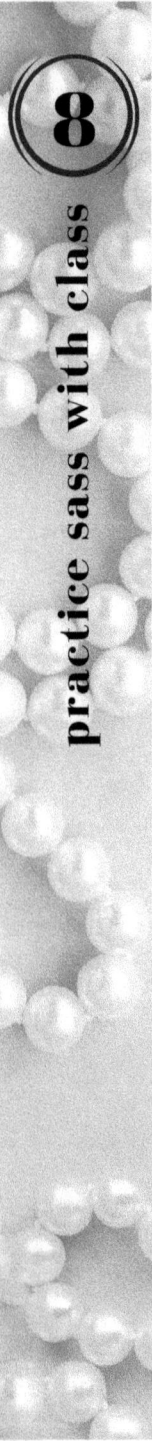

8

practice sass with class

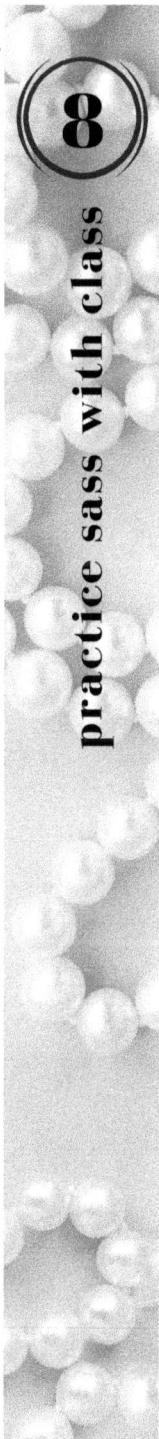

date _____

practice sass with class

Beverly Ingle

RULE #9
rivalries belong on the gridiron

In the South, every Saturday during the fall is Game Day.
Yes, capitalized. Game. Day. Don't ask what sport, because there's
only one that really matters: College Football.

There are few things more fun – or more intense – than a
college football game, especially one between rivals. Game days are
perfect occasions for a Modern Belle to indulge in two of her favorite
activities: dressing up and hosting a party. However, game day parties
are tailgates and dressing up is dictated by her favorite school's
colors. And while she readily abides the expected social rules and
norms, game days are when a belle unabashedly allows herself to get
rowdy. And getting rowdy usually means getting loud. Really loud.

It's no surprise that while the rowdiness is fueled by a belle's
favorite cocktail, it's her school fight song that triggers the truly out-
of-character response. And when it comes to rivalries, that college
fight song brings out the ribald side of a belle and her fellow fans. I
know of which I write. I'm a proud alumna of the University of Texas;
I bleed burnt orange. The lyrics of our fight song actually speak to our
long-standing, historic rivalry with Texas A&M University. However,
when UT plays its other major rival, the University of Oklahoma, fans
have been known to change the lyrics up a bit just for them. (Those

RULE #9
rivalries belong on the gridiron

lyrics are too tacky to share here.) Good Lord, there are some epic rivalries in the South: Georgia vs. Florida, Clemson vs. South Carolina, Mississippi State vs. Ole Miss, LSU vs. Alabama, and Alabama vs., well, everybody. The intensity of these games is nearly impossible to describe to an outsider. Believe me, I tried to no avail. It wasn't until I dragged my now-ex-husband to a UT vs. OU game that he finally understood. He turned to look at me and said, "This isn't a game. This is war!" No truer words were ever spoken.

Indulging in Game Day rivalries is a great outlet for some of a Modern Belle's energy since, sadly, for far too long rivalries in a belle's life were limited to other women. How twisted is that?! For centuries, when we should have been supporting one another and having each other's back, society was pitting us against each other. The ingénue competing for a man's attention. The Junior League members jockeying for the presidency. The mother-in-law. Consider what we could have accomplished had we banded together much earlier!

While Game Day rivalries run deep through generations of Southerners, the kind of rivalries among women that we grew up with need to become a thing of the past. Instead of competing for a man, compete for a CEO position. Work together to get more diverse representation on boards of directors instead of undermining each other and settling for just one board position. And try to remember that you may one day be a mother-in-law, too, and try to show some compassion ... unless she cheers for your school's rival, then all bets are off.

your turn ...

rivalries belong on the gridiron

Consider the rivalries you may have had or currently have. Why did or do they exist? What are you getting from them that adds to your life? How can you look at that rival-rich relationship differently so everyone benefits?

9

rivalries belong on the gridiron

date _____

rivalries belong on the gridiron

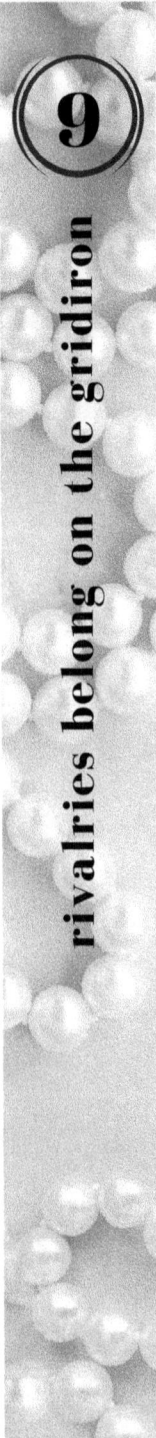

9

rivalries belong on the gridiron

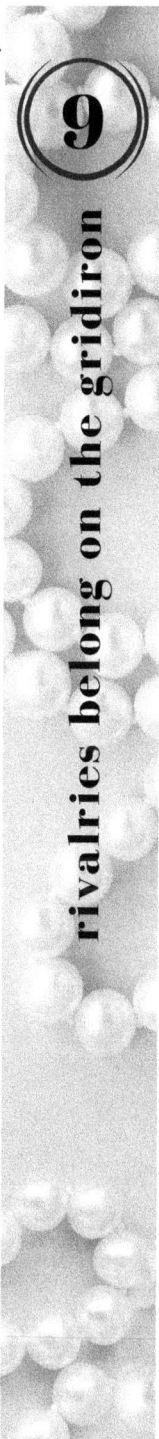

date _____

rivalries belong on the gridiron

RULE #10
friendships needed

I've heard interesting speculation about how friendships between Southern women are born. I've overheard someone insisting that at a certain upper echelon of society, friendships are arranged much like marriages used to be. As if because the Smiths and the Joneses run in the same elite social circle, then their children must of course be BFFs. I've heard the tired trope on the inability of friendships to cross Southern socio-economic or racial lines being perpetuated without any substance to support the claim. And I've heard the equally tired trope of the rebellious belle breaking ranks and befriending a girl who, for all intents and purposes, is her exact opposite in style, influence and race.

To the Modern Belle, the idea of these types of friendships are laughable, because they are contrary to their own experiences.

No longer does geography have such a strong effect on how Modern Belles develop friendships. The style of upbringing? Yes, to a degree. In the South, belles are raised to be polite, pleasant and approachable. We Modern Belles are expected to be able to hold our own in conversation, chat with everyone – especially anyone getting left on the fringes of the gathering – show and voice appreciation to our hosts, and reciprocate the hospitality whenever possible.

RULE #10
friendships needed

These social norms quickly establish connections and undoubtedly facilitate the opportunity for friendships.

While all of that is well and good, it's shared interests and genuine affection that ground the best friendships. Think bonding and laughter, compatible life goals and silliness. For some belles, more traditional organizations like The Junior League, the Daughters of the American Revolution or any number of similarly established groups fill the bill. For others, not so much. And that's OK. Membership in "The Organizations" to which our mothers belonged isn't a prerequisite to happiness, and may indeed represent an outdated and unwelcome social contract. Case in point...

As a newly minted adult, I firmly believed that my next step in creating friendships would be made through joining the Junior League. While I have friends who had wonderful experiences and made life-long friends while serving as members, my experience was the opposite. I was kicked out. I kind of wear that stigma as a badge of honor, now. Let me explain why.

At the time this all went down, I was early in a pregnancy with triplets. I was horribly sick one morning and couldn't attend a scheduled shift at a fundraiser. Per the rules and regs, I was to find a replacement for my shift or be penalized with a $150 fine. Since I was a new member, I had no one – not a friend or even an acquaintance – who I could call to fill my spot, nor did I have the strength to chase down a stranger for help. After the fundraising event came my reckoning.

I had already committed to serving the next year as the editor for my League's annual magazine, a role that would equate to providing thousands of dollars of my professional talent and time. I was excited

RULE #10
friendships needed

about the opportunity and eager to serve. Until I got The Phone Call from the membership director of our board. I owed $150 for my missed shift.

Aside from the illness that kept me from fulfilling my shift, I had recently delivered twins prematurely (we had lost the triplet at 11 weeks) and was strapped financially with steep medical bills. The $150 fine was prohibitive. Extenuating circumstances be damned, I was expected to pay my fine before assuming my new responsibilities. Normally, I'm a rule follower, when a rule makes sense. In my circumstance, this rule didn't.

Although I advocated for myself and explained my situation with all transparency, the board wouldn't be swayed. In fact, the president told me that I apparently didn't fully understand the mission of the League, to which I questioned was it not to support women in their endeavors to improve their lives and the lives of those around them? In the end, rather than make an exception and benefit from my future service, I was dismissed.

Apparently, Junior League would not be my breeding ground for adult friendships.

For the Modern Belle, finding her circle of BFFs is as easy – or as difficult – as following her heart. As I learned, joining organizations because we are legacies or because it's THE organization to belong to isn't always the right choice. Rather, we connect with other women who feel or think in similar ways and who share the same passions and moral guidelines. That's the first step to finding friends who share our quirky sense of humor, taste in TV shows and indulgent sweet tooth. And if we keep our eyes open, we'll discover with sheer delight the women who we know, at a gut-instinct level, will be the ones we'll call

RULE #10
friendships needed

when it hits the fan.

It's just as important to truly understand that the best of friends don't have to be in constant contact with one another to be considered close. I think more of us Modern Belles have come to terms with this fact: Life is just too chaotic to keep track of who contacted whom last. Friendships are not about keeping score, and to keep from reaching out to someone because it's the other's turn to initiate contact isn't just silly, it's hurtful.

Life's pace doesn't always allow for a consistent rhythm of contact and togetherness, and that's ok. The best friendships truly are those that no matter how much time might pass, you pick up right where you left off. Who wouldn't want that kind of ROI on one's time?! I have several of these friends, and they are more valuable to me than gold. These kinds of friendships ooze with love yet are low-maintenance. While some of them live thousands of miles away, they feel as close as if they were next door, and I know that if I need them, I just have to say the word. They know they can do same with me. They are my tribe, and I am all the better for them.

your turn ...

friendships needed

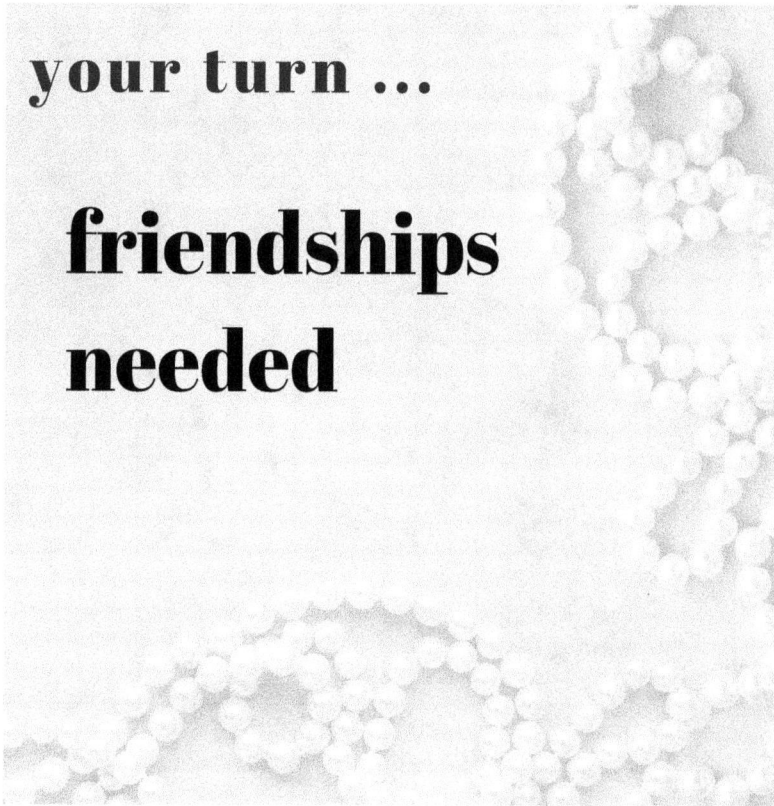

Think about your friendships in all their various shapes and types. Do they each add value to your life? Do any of them feel like a drain?

Take note of who among your friends are the ones you would call if something horrible happened in your life. Would you drop everything to help them if you could? Would they do the same for you?

friendships needed

date _____

date _____

friendships needed

friendships needed

date _____

date _____

friendships needed

Stay connected to
the 10 Little Rules Community

Like and Follow our Facebook
page at facebook.com/10LittleRules
for ongoing support and discussion on
how to apply these books to living your best life

Visit our website for updates
at www.10littlerules.com

Books in the 10 Little Rules series:
10 Little Rules for a Blissy Life by Carol Pearson
10 Little Rules for Your Creative Soul by Rita Long
10 Little Rules of Hank by Wendy Price
10 Little Rules for Finding Your Truth by Micki Beach
10 Little Rules for Mermaids by Amy Hege Atwell
10 Little Rules for the Modern South Belle by Beverly Ingle

Watch for more 10 Little Rules books launching soon!

www.ingramcontent.com/pod-product-compliance
Lightning Source LLC
Chambersburg PA
CBHW062103270326
41931CB00013B/3193